I0502997

Welcome Book for Vacation Rentals

Property Location

_____

Name of Vacation Rental:

Property Address:

Welcome Book for Guests

Upon arrival please have each member of your party review this Welcome Book.

Please keep it on the counter in a place that is visible to you and your party so it is easily accessible to you as you need it. It contains pertinent information about this unit and specifically designed to help make your stay more enjoyable. It includes the following pages:

- Welcome Page.
- Contact information.
- Emergency telephone numbers and addresses and where to find a first aid kit in this unit.
- Helpful instructions for electronics in this unit.
- Parking Instructions - Lot Diagram.
- Renter's Rules Agreement.
- Pet Rules:
- Pool Rules
- Local Attractions.
- Restaurants, telephone numbers, addresses and menus.
- Local Marinas
- Ski Areas.
- Transportation Options
- Day of Departure: Instructions on where to leave key, etc.
- Owner's Notes
- Helpful Notes from Guests
- Reviews from Guests

Emergency Contact person and Phone Number:

Name of Vacation Rental:

Property Address:

Welcome to Our Vacation Home

Thank you for choosing our vacation home for you and your party. We take special pride in keeping our home immaculate and as *comfortable* as possible for our guests.

We sincerely appreciate your leaving our unit as clean as it was upon your arrival.

Please be courteous about using the utilities: Do not leave the air conditioner or electrical appliances on when leaving the premises, for safety, environmental and economical reasons.

Kitchen: Please keep counters, refrigerator, stove and sink clean.

Bathrooms: Please keep clean and dry.

Cleaning products are located under each sink for your convenience.

If you have any questions whatsoever, please feel free to contact us.

We hope your stay is enjoyable. We look forward to your return!

Sincerely,

_____

Owner

Emergency Contact person and Phone Number:

Name of Vacation Rental:

Property Address:

Contact Information

Owner's Telephone Numbers:

Home Telephone No: _____

Cellular No: _____

Office Telephone No: _____

Housekeeper:

(House Keeping Services provided at additional cost)

Name: _____

Telephone No: _____

Maintenance Person:

Name: _____

Telephone No: _____

Additional Information:

Gas Station: _____

Directions: _____

Grocery Store: _____

Directions: _____

ATM Machine _____

Directions: _____

_____

Emergency Contact person and Phone Number:

Name of Vacation Rental:

Property Address:

<u>Emergency Information:</u>

Fire Department: _____

Police Department: _____

Poison Control Center: _____

Hospital:

Hospital Name: _____

Address: _____

Telephone No: _____

First Aid Kit Location in House: _____

Emergency Contact person and Phone Number:

Name of Vacation Rental:

Property Address:

Helpful Instructions

- <u>Fireplace Instructions:</u>

  Use fire wood located at _____. Flue needs to be open. The handle is marked to open and close.

- <u>Wood Stove:</u>

  The Wood Stove should not be used, unless you have experience with this type of stove. Do not store wood inside of unit. Keep the wood _____.

- <u>Skis:</u>

  Please keep skis_____.

- <u>Gas Grill:</u>

  The gas grill is available for your convenience. Please keep it clean and shut off gas when not in use.

- <u>Cable/Satellite TV Instructions:</u>

  _____

- <u>DVD Player Instructions:</u>

  _____

- <u>Internet Services Instructions:</u>

  _____

- <u>Additional Electronics Instructions:</u>

  _____

_____

Emergency Contact person and Phone Number:

Name of Vacation Rental:

Property Address:

Parking Instructions

Overnight Guests Parking Space Number and Location:

_____

Day Visitor's Parking Space Location:

_____

Number of parking spaces available on premises: _____

Parking stickers are necessary for guests.   Yes____ No____

Additional Notes pertaining to Parking:

_____
_____
_____
_____
_____

*Add Diagram of Parking Area

_____

Emergency Contact person and Phone Number:

Name of Vacation Rental:

Property Address:

RENTAL RULES AND REGULATIONS

Beach Rules

- Renters shall refrain from using loud and abusive language and noise levels at all hours of the day. Outdoor activities shall cease after _____pm
- Barb-que Grills shall only be used _____.
- All trash must be left _____.
- Pets allowed/not allowed on the premises by renters.
- The beach area shall be used exclusively for swimming and associated activities.
- Open fires are/ are not permitted on the beach.
- Trash shall not be left on the beach at any time.
- Parents shall attend the beach with children to supervise their activities.
- Camping is allowed/not allowed on the beach.
- Beach Towels can/cannot be hung over deck railing.
- Renters can/cannot use the docks for loading and unloading passengers.

Additional Rules and Regulations:

_____
_____
_____
_____
_____

Guest(s) acknowledges he/she has read the rules and regulations and agrees to abide by them.

Renter's Signature_____Date_____

Print_____

Renter's Signature_____Date_____

Print_____

_____

Emergency Contact person and Phone Number:

Name of Vacation Rental:

Property Address:

Standard Pet Policies and Guidelines

- Pets weighing less than _____pounds are welcome with the exception of:_____

  _____

- Proper medical certification specifying that all vaccinations are up to date must be available upon request.

- Pets may/may not be left alone in unit. However, if you leave the premises with your pet unattended in the unit, the pet must be in a crate or pet carrier while you are gone.

- Pets are not allowed in the public areas such as:

  _____

  _____

- Pets must be on a controllable leash at all times when outside the unit.

- Renters must walk their pets in designated walk areas such as_____

  _____ and are responsible for picking up after their pet in and around the premises at all times.

- House Keeping Service – The pet must be removed from the unit prior to housekeeping services.

_____

Emergency Contact person and Phone Number:

Name of Vacation Rental:

Property Address:

Pool Rules

Pool Opens at: _____

Pool Closes at: _____

Children under the age of _____ must be accompanied by an adult in the pool.

Swimsuits, swim-diapers or swim trunks only – no shorts, t-shirts, diapers, thongs, etc.

Please shower before entering pool.

No diving, no running, horseplay or rough play.

No cuts, open sores, bandages or infectious diseases.

No smoking, eating, drinking, except in designated areas such as:

_____.

No glass containers. No alcoholic beverages.

No profanity.

No animals or pets, except seeing-eye dogs and K-9 officers.

No flotation devices, except U.S. Coast Guard approved lifejackets.

Additional Information: _____

_____

_____

Name of Vacation Rental:

Property Address:

<u>Local Attractions</u>

Beaches, Golf Resorts, Theatre, Shopping outlets, Amusement Parks, Site Seeing Roads, Hiking Trails, Snowmobile Trails, Skiing areas, Movie Theater, etc.

Name: _____

Address: _____

Phone No: _____

Activities: _____

Best for Ages: _____

Directions: _____

Name: _____

Address: _____

Phone No: _____

Activities: _____

Best for Ages: _____

Directions: _____

Name: _____

Address: _____

Phone No: _____

Activities: _____

Best for Ages: _____

Emergency Contact person and Phone Number:

Name of Vacation Rental:

Property Address:

Local Attractions

Beaches, Golf Resorts, Theatre, Shopping outlets, Amusement Parks, Site Seeing Roads, Hiking Trails, Snowmobile Trails, Skiing areas, Movie Theater, etc.

Name: _____

Address: _____

Phone No: _____

Activities: _____

Best for Ages: _____

Directions: _____

Name: _____

Address: _____

Phone No: _____

Activities: _____

Best for Ages: _____

Directions: _____

Name: _____

Address: _____

Phone No: _____

Activities: _____

Best for Ages: _____

_____

Emergency Contact person and Phone Number:

Name of Vacation Rental:

Property Address:

Local Attractions

Beaches, Golf Resorts, Theatre, Shopping outlets, Amusement Parks, Site Seeing Roads, Hiking Trails, Snowmobile Trails, Skiing areas, Movie Theater, etc.

Name: _____

Address: _____

Phone No: _____

Activities: _____

Best for Ages: _____

Directions: _____

Name: _____

Address: _____

Phone No: _____

Activities: _____

Best for Ages: _____

Directions: _____

Name: _____

Address: _____

Phone No: _____

Activities: _____

Best for Ages: _____

_____

Emergency Contact person and Phone Number:

Name of Vacation Rental:

Property Address:

Restaurants

Fine Dining:

Name: _____

Address: _____

Phone No: _____

Type of Food: _____

Directions: _____

Name: _____

Address: _____

Phone No: _____

Type of Food: _____

Directions: _____

Name: _____

Address: _____

Phone No: _____

Type of Food: _____

Directions: _____

_____

Emergency Contact person and Phone Number:

Name of Vacation Rental:

Property Address:

Casual Dining:

Name: _____

Address: _____

Phone No: _____

Type of Food: _____

Directions: _____

Name: _____

Address: _____

Phone No: _____

Type of Food: _____

Directions: _____

Name: _____

Address: _____

Phone No: _____

Type of Food: _____

Directions: _____

Emergency Contact person and Phone Number:

Name of Vacation Rental:

Property Address:

Casual Lounge:

Name: _____

Address: _____

Phone No: _____

Type of Food: _____

Directions: _____

Name: _____

Address: _____

Phone No: _____

Type of Food: _____

Directions: _____

Name: _____

Address: _____

Phone No: _____

Type of Food: _____

Directions: _____

Emergency Contact person and Phone Number:

Name of Vacation Rental:

Property Address:

<u>Music and Dancing:</u>

Name: _____

Address: _____

Phone No: _____

Type of Food: _____

Directions: _____

Name: _____

Address: _____

Phone No: _____

Type of Food: _____

Directions: _____

Name: _____

Address: _____

Phone No: _____

Type of Food: _____

Directions: _____

_____

Emergency Contact person and Phone Number:

Name of Vacation Rental:

Property Address:

<u>Local Marina</u>

Rentals: Pontoon Boat, Jet Skis, Paddle Boat, Wave Runner, Canoes, Snorkel Equipment, Water Ski etc.

Name: _____

Address: _____

Phone No: _____

Type of Rentals: _____

Directions: _____

Name: _____

Address: _____

Phone No: _____

Type of Rentals: _____

Directions: _____

Name: _____

Address: _____

Phone No: _____

Type of Rentals: _____

Directions: _____

_____

Emergency Contact person and Phone Number:

Name of Vacation Rental:

Property Address:

Ski Areas

Rentals: Snow Boards, Downhill Skis, Snow Shoes, Snow Tubes, Cross Country Skis, etc.

Name: _____

Address: _____

Phone No: _____

Type of Rentals: _____

Directions: _____

Name: _____

Address: _____

Phone No: _____

Type of Rentals: _____

Directions: _____

Name: _____

Address: _____

Phone No: _____

Type of Rentals: _____

Directions: _____

_____

Emergency Contact person and Phone Number:

Name of Vacation Rental:

Property Address:

<u>**Transportation Options**</u>

Taxi & Shuttle Services: _____

_____

Bus Routes: _____

_____

Car Rentals: _____

_____

Airports and Train Stations: _____

_____

Area Maps: _____

_____

Emergency Contact person and Phone Number:

Name of Vacation Rental:

Property Address:

Day of Departure

- Please wash all used linens and towels. If you cannot finish cleaning all towels and sheets, please leave them in the laundry room before your departure.
- Please leave all bathrooms clean and dry.
- Please do not leave dirty dishes in dishwasher.
- Please leave thermostat on _____degrees.
- Shut off all lights in each room.
- Main water valve must be turned on/off prior to leaving the unit.
- All windows and outside doors should be closed and locked.
- All blinds should be left open/closed at departure.
- All trash should be emptied before your departure.
- Please leave key _____.
- Time of Departure: _____am./pm.
- Please understand another party may be arriving shortly after your departure.

If you would like to reserve this same time period next year, please let me know as soon as possible since this is our high-demand season and often books quickly.

Hope you to see you again next year!

Sincerely,

_____

Owner

_____

Emergency Contact person and Phone Number:

Name of Vacation Rental:

Property Address:

Owner's NOTES:

Name of Vacation Rental:

_____

Emergency Contact person and Phone Number:

Name of Vacation Rental:

Property Address:

Helpful NOTES from Guests:

_____

Emergency Contact person and Phone Number:

Name of Vacation Rental:

Property Address:

Helpful NOTES from Guests:

Name of Vacation Rental:

_____

Emergency Contact person and Phone Number:

Name of Vacation Rental:

Property Address:

Reviews from Guests:

Name of Vacation Rental:

Emergency Contact person and Phone Number:

Name of Vacation Rental:

Property Address:

Reviews from Guests:

Name of Vacation Rental:

_____

Emergency Contact person and Phone Number:

Name of Vacation Rental:

Property Address:

_____

Emergency Contact person and Phone Number:

www.ingramcontent.com/pod-product-compliance
Lightning Source LLC
Chambersburg PA
CBHW082306200526

45168CB00018B/3422

* 9 7 8 1 5 0 8 5 0 1 8 3 1 *